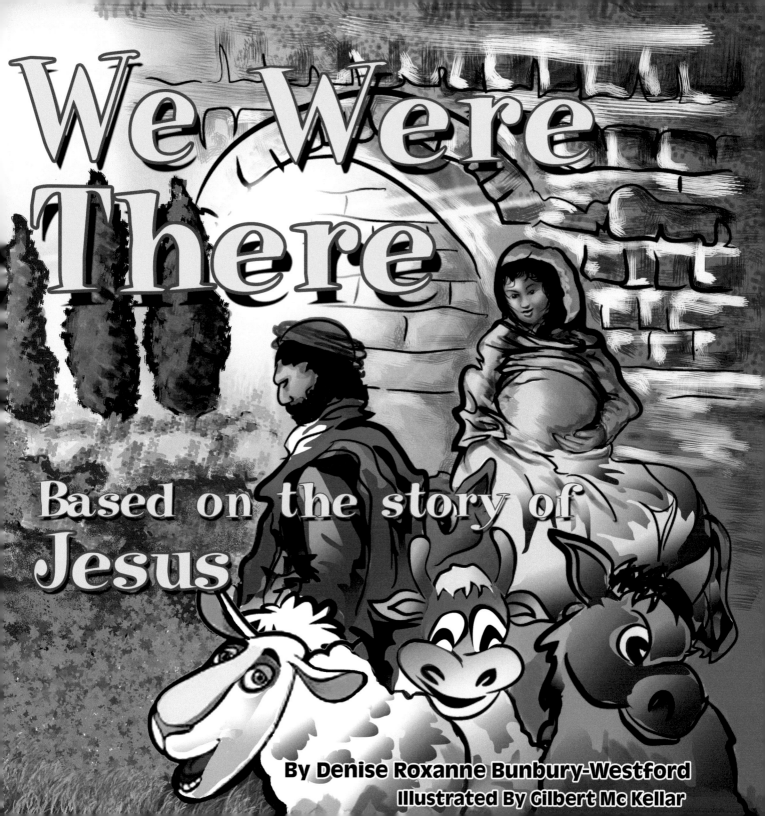

We Were There

Based on the story of Jesus

By Denise Roxanne Bunbury-Westford

Illustrated By Gilbert Mc Kellar

Mandy, Peggy and Millie were living a normal life in the town of Nazareth
until the night their master brought two humans,
Mary and Joseph into their home.
Join them as they tell how God chose their stable
to be the birthplace of a special baby boy, 'Jesus'.

We wanted to play a game with you.
So in the story Peggy, Millie and I
made a deliberate boo boo.
Can you find it?

Once there was a King in a place called Rome. He wanted everyone in the country to be counted. So he told them to go back to the town where they were born.

Lots of people were coming to Nazareth,
the town where we - me, Mandy (the sheep)
Peggy (the donkey) and Millie (the cow), lived.
Everyone needed a place to stay.
The hotels were filling up fast.

Soon it started to get dark. Our master brought us
into the stable to settle down for the night.
All was quiet. Suddenly, with a burst of light,
the stable door opened! My master came in with
a couple. He called the man Joseph, and the woman,
Mary. Mary was holding her stomach.
She looked as though she was in pain.

We wondered why the master had brought them into the stable. He spoke to the couple. Then he told us to move to the back of the stable.

He then took a trough and put some hay in it. Joseph cleared a spot on the floor of the stable and spread some blankets the master had given him. Mary lay down and he lay next to her.

About twenty minutes later Mary sat up. Joseph was still sleeping. She shook him and woke him up. She said something to him.

He jumped up and ran towards the master's house. A few minutes later he and the master came back. A lady in a white dress was with them. She spoke to Mary and told her to lie down. We could not see what was happening. After what seemed like forever, we heard a baby crying.

The lady put the baby in the trough.
Joseph kneeled down and started to pray.
Tears were rolling down his cheeks. He turned to
the master and told him that the baby's name was
Jesus. We tried to draw closer to see the baby.
It was a boy! He was smiling and his face seemed
bright like rays of sunshine.

Almost immediately, we heard singing in the distance. My master opened the stable door. Up in the sky we saw a bright light. It sent rays straight to the stable where the baby was. In the midst of the light we saw what looked like humans with wings. They were singing, "Glory to God in the highest! Peace on earth and goodwill toward men!" We realized that this was a very special baby. Peggy, Millie and I looked at each other.

We were happy that God chose our stable for him to be born. It was a night we would never forget! We were so excited we could not go back to sleep. We couldn't wait for morning to tell the other animals of our unusual adventure. Now they will surely stop making jokes about our home.

Printed in the United States
By Bookmasters